JAZZ RHYTHM
AND THE
IMPROVISED LINE

JAZZ RHYTHM AND THE IMPROVISED LINE

Jazz Improvisation II

John Mehegan

*Instructor in Jazz Improvisation,
Juilliard School of Music*

Published by
WATSON-GUPTILL PUBLICATIONS
New York

Exclusive Distributor to the Music Trade
AMSCO MUSIC PUBLISHING COMPANY
33 West 60th Street, New York 10023

Exclusive Distributor to the Book Trade
SIMON AND SCHUSTER
New York

To Doris, Carey, and Gretchen

CONTENTS

PREFACE

The reader's first thought upon scanning this might well be: "Why was a song writer asked to write this preface?" Well now, if I may quote John Mehegan's inscription to me in his brilliant first volume of JAZZ IMPROVISATION — "To Harold Arlen, whose tunes are a source of inspiration to all jazz men" — it would seem that there is some contingent area where song writers and jazz musicians meet to draw from a common source. Perhaps this wellspring is the blues, which, I am told, finds its home in some of my music. I am pleased to discover that at times my music may act as an emissary in the fascinating conversation which occurs between the jazz musician and his audience.

Yes, I'm human enough to take pride in his inscription, but *more than that* it reveals the absolute truth about the collaboration of composers and improvisors. One may improvise to his heart's content, but the listener cannot fully appreciate the magic of the stylists and their improvisations unless they take flight around a theme or melody with which the listener is already familiar. Only then is their work understood, and all their flights take on a new meaning when they have a base, or perhaps I should say "bass," to depart from and come home to.

It was an improvisation of a traditional vamp that was responsible for my first hit, "Get Happy." That melody has been the base for many original inventions, and I bow to the superb talents of the men in this volume who have collaborated (although they may not know it) with many a song writer in keeping their songs interestingly alive. Let no one who thinks he knows anything about jazz improvisation or the various piano styles that have evolved through the years slough off this volume as something to rest in a dusty archive. Jazz is distinguished by its urgent vitality, and it seems to me that the author has captured this special quality of jazz by choosing the individualists — the innovators; for in every generation there are those who follow and the blessed few who lead.

It is quite unusual to find one so devoted, knowledgeable, and unstinting as John Mehegan in his efforts to bring musical order to this most driving, unique, and universal art form so lovingly shared by so many.

Harold Arlen
New York City
1962

NOTE

The Publisher wishes to express his appreciation to Lewis Roth for his advice and assistance in the preparation of this book.

INTRODUCTION

Volume II of *Jazz Improvisation* deals with the schematic history of two important facets of jazz:

1. Rhythm
2. The improvised line

It is in the areas of rhythm that the jazzman has achieved his most magnificent expression; it is in the improvised line that he has given this rhythm vitality and meaning. As the jazz musician calls forth his resources of imagination, technique, and taste to generate that elusive quality called *swing*, he also learns that the sum total of the resources he deals with eventually are transformed into the common denominator of all jazz — rhythm. Volume I of *Jazz Improvisation* explored the tonal aspects of this problem. The present volume deals first with the rhythmic genesis of improvisation, and second with reproductions of outstanding recordings created by jazz musicians over the past thirty-five years. Various schematic outlines trace the evolution of jazz rhythm, harmony, and the improvised line.

The subject of jazz rhythm has been of major concern to all jazzmen throughout the history of the art form. Jazzmen usually refer to jazz rhythm in all its manifestations as *time*. *Time* encompasses all of the aspects of tempo, beat, pulse, and, above all, the elusive element called *swing*. For one jazzman to acknowledge that another jazzman *swings* is to confer the highest accolade. What is *swing?* Tempo may be metronomically determined; pulse and meter rest within the notation of a composition; but the *swing* or lack of *swing* of a performance is very difficult to evaluate objectively.

The performance of a Bach Fugue, a Strauss waltz, a Sousa march, or a rhythm and blues recording — each can be said to *swing* within its own context. The problem of evaluating the *swing* of a jazz performance lies in recognizing the multiple levels of pulsation which must converge in the performance to create *swing*.

MELODIC SWING:

The presence or absence of *swing* in an improvised line is determined by the following factors:

1. Relationship of improvising units (eighth, sixteenth, thirty-second notes) to the basic beat.
2. Punctuation in relation to stresses within the bar.
3. Punctuation in relation to the bar-line.

9

4. Constant transitions from unit to unit (eighth, sixteenth, eighth-note triplet to thirty-second, etc.) to sustain melodic interest.

5. Direction changes within a phrase in order to avoid one-directional "runs."

6. Accent placements capable of falling at any point of opposition to the basic pulse.

7. Interesting interval textures employing all units of the interval span from the minor second to the major ninth.

8. Constant tonal transitions from release (modal) to tension (non-modal) or the opposite transition (tension to release). The resulting line, by constantly alternating between these two factors, will avoid the oppressive monotony of total release (modal) or total tension (non-modal). It is well to remember that the ear (like all sensory organs) functions on a premise of opposition, i.e. release is non-tension, tension is non-release. One can only exist effectively by the presence of the other.

9. Constant transitions between the basic quality tones of a chord (root, third, fifth, and seventh) and the ornamental tones (ninth, eleventh, and thirteenth).

10. Use of sequence, retrograde motion, diminution, and augmentation to enhance musical order.

11. Use of dynamics in order to clearly establish the rise and fall of musical sentences.

12. Contrasting touch or tonal timbres in order to achieve an emotional palette.

HARMONIC SWING:

The *swing* of a harmonic progression or chord chart can hardly be underestimated, since it is the transmission belt of any jazz performance. Harmonic *swing* is essentially based upon the procession of patterns appearing in a tune. (See Volume I, Lesson 62, 63, 64). These circles of fifths, diatonic and chromatic patterns have all evolved from the Baroque, Classical, and Romantic traditions and represent a distillation of the harmonic designs most conducive to a propelling beat. A badly organized chord chart may quite easily dispel the effectiveness of a jazz performance that might otherwise (melodically and rhythmically) possess the necessary qualifications of *swing*. The circle of fifths, of course, takes precedence over either diatonic or chromatic designs in creating harmonic *swing*. The reason for this lies in a fundamental fact of all tonality — namely that the basic cadence design of the circle of fifths (II - V - I) is the most effective means of establishing harmonic tension, which demands an inevitable resolution. Orderly diatonic and chromatic patterns act primarily as connective material joining the circle of fifths.

Chromatic harmonic designs usually possess the tension of inevitable resolution more than diatonic patterns and are often employed as "substitute" structures for the circle of fifths: For instance:

Circle pattern: III - VIx - II - V - I

Chromatic substitute: III - ♭IIIx - II - ♭IIx - I

The subject of "substitute" chords is one that consumes the interest of many immature jazz musicians, who seem to feel that the acquisition of a few "substitute" chords will automatically transform them into developed performers. The term "substitute" as used by these people actually means the *correct* chords for a jazz chart, as opposed to the *incorrect* chords often appearing in sheet music or numerous "fake" books. This whole idea is, of course, an illusory one that only at best can "patch up" an otherwise faltering array of resources. The only authentic "substitute" chord is the chromatic substitute for the circle of fifths (♭IIIx for VIx), the so-called "augmented fourth substitute." A correct chord cannot under any circumstances be considered a "substitute" for an incorrect chord.

RHYTHMIC SWING:

Music theorists have usually centered their interest upon the rhythmic aspects of jazz, since they have quite correctly established that the jazzman has not been an innovator in the areas of harmony and melody. In the realm of voicing existing harmonic materials, jazz pianists have been singularly inventive (i.e. Tatum, Wilson, Powell, and Shearing). But for the most part jazzmen have been content to borrow their tonal resources from such diverse areas as Lutheran hymns and Stravinsky's *Sacre du Printemps*.

As indicated in the introductory notes to Volume I, the *rhythmic engine* found in all jazz, regardless of period or style, is a form of florid counterpoint involving three levels of time. Each level represents one of the three basic elements of all music:

♪ — melodic time

𝅗𝅥 — harmonic time

♩ — rhythmic time

As indicated in Volume I and further explored in the present volume, the melodic and harmonic units both employ a number of variables ranging on the melodic level from ♩ to ♬ and on the harmonic level from ♩ to ◯◠◯◠◯◠◯ It is in the creative use of these variables that the ordinary harmonic and rhythmic resources of jazz are transformed into the sensuality, the lyricism, the pathos, and the savagery of the art form.

Probably the most representative point of view of the serious musician toward the question of jazz rhythm has been expressed by Igor Stravinsky*. Responding to an inquiry by Robert Craft concerning his attitude toward jazz, Stravinsky expressed an admiration tinged with affection for the virtuosity of jazz musicians. He also pointed out that jazz is by far the finest form of popular musical culture in America today. One curious comment of Stravinsky's which seemed to reveal his attitude toward jazz rhythm, was his statement that jazz rhythm did not "really exist" since it possessed neither "proportion" nor "relaxation."

Actually, jazz rhythm falls into two basic segments:

SUPERSTRUCTURE (melodic and harmonic units and
     their variables)

SUBSTRATUM (basic pulse or beat)

True, the basic pulse or beat, by definition, is without "proportion" or "relaxation;" however, the *superstructure* of melodic and harmonic variables is, by definition, constantly subject to the identical concepts of "proportion" and "relaxation" that prevail in serious music. The fact that these levels of "proportion" and "relaxation" are not always maintained is part of the relentless discipline of the art form, which, as in all art forms, takes its toll of faltering heros. This can never in any way repudiate the absolutes (relative to style and period) established by such master figures as Armstrong, Beiderbecke, Hawkins, Goodman, Tatum, Parker and Powell.

This brings us to the second section of this present volume dealing with a schematic history of the improvised line.

The final and most severe commitment of the jazz musician is to "blow a line" on the changes of a tune. This line should represent an imaginative design built upon the rhythmic, harmonic, and melodic inflections implicit in the composition. Volume II will document some of the greatest lines played in the thirty-five years from 1923 to 1958.

Each period produces its own monumental achievements of the improvised line, which in time become a point of departure for succeeding generations. For convenience, it is well to use the following period breakdown.

---

*Igor Stravinsky and Robert Craft, *Conversations with Igor Stravinsky* (Garden City, New York: Doubleday & Co., 1959).

ARCHAIC: 1875-1915
  gospel songs
  work songs
  hollers
  medicine shows
  minstrels
  ragtime
  blues

NEW ORLEANS: 1915-1925
  Louis Armstrong
  King Oliver
  Nick LaRocca
  Jelly Roll Morton
  Kid Ory
  Honoré Dutrey
  Leon Rapallo
  Johnny Dodds
  Jimmie Noone
  Bessie Smith

CHICAGO: NEW YORK: 1925-1935
  Earl Hines
  James P. Johnson
  Fats Waller
  Bix Beiderbecke
  Miff Mole
  Jack Teagarden
  Frank Teschemacher
  Pee Wee Russell
  Bud Freeman
  Eddie Lang
  Jimmy Harrison
  Tommy Ladnier

SWING: 1935-1940
  Art Tatum
  Teddy Wilson
  Roy Eldridge

Bunny Berigan
Vic Dickenson
Benny Goodman
Benny Carter
Johnny Hodges
Coleman Hawkins
Chu Berry
Ben Webster
Harry Carney
Charlie Christian
Django Reinhardt
Red Norvo
Hershel Evans

EARLY PROGRESSIVES: 1940-1948
  Bud Powell
  Dizzy Gillespie
  Miles Davis
  Bill Harris
  Charlie Parker
  J. J. Johnson
  Stan Hasselgard
  Lester Young
  Serge Chaloff

LATER PROGRESSIVES: 1948-1958
  Horace Silver
  Oscar Peterson
  Hampton Hawes
  Chet Baker
  Clifford Brown
  Bob Brookmeyer
  Lee Konitz
  John Coltrane
  Gerry Mulligan
  Tal Farlow
  George Shearing
  Stan Getz
  Milt Jackson

Instruments represented in the above outline include trumpet; piano; trombone; alto, tenor, and baritone saxophones; clarinet; xylophone; vibraphone; and the human voice. Instruments auxiliary to the improvised line (bass, drums, etc.) and those upon which no major developments have occurred (flute, organ, etc.) have been omitted.

That this list of the melodic giants of jazz is incomplete is immediately obvious to even the casual reader. Most people naturally feel that anyone they like is very good and a candidate for the jazz Valhalla, but the exigencies of history are fortunately a little more demanding, primarily because in retrospect the contribution is distilled from the performance.

The average listener is rightfully concerned with the immediate performance and has little patience or interest in the eventual, dry summing-up. The author is solely responsible for the arbitrary selections herein, and he feels that the reader rightfully deserves some explanation of the pitfalls, whimsies, and, above all, prejudices of the author.

First, it is believed in this quarter that the lyrical line abounding in sensitive melodies and harmonic inflection, in addition to that elusive element *swing*, is the most demanding, most rare, and most important element in jazz. Respectfully excluded are all types of styles based upon slurs, growls, wa-waing, honking, or slap-tongue. Furthermore, styles employing in an essential way the use of plungers, half-valve, mutes, or hats expressing some degree of bathos, onomatopoea, or some such figures of musical speech, have been omitted on the grounds of being either too specific or too topical.

Many melodic instruments upon which jazz can be played have been ignored on the basic grounds that no major achievement has been initially presented on such instruments and also on the further basis that just as there are major and minor figures in jazz, so there are major and minor instruments, and major figures tend to play major instruments probably because they offer a wider spectrum of sound and emotion.

In the labyrinthian maze of the jazz discography, which had its inception in 1921 and has flourished into a multi-million dollar industry, the historian faces a tremendous task of ferreting out some continuity of development in the art form. Who are the major figures, the minor figures, the innovators, the consolidators, the creators, the contributors, the popularizers, the recreators? What is the mainstream; which are the tributaries? Where are the lines of influence? For one thing, the lines of influence crisscross from one instrument to another: Louis Armstrong to Earl Hines; Benny Carter to Teddy Wilson; Art Tatum to Charlie Parker; Charlie Parker to Bud Powell; Horace Silver to Chet Baker.

Actually, new, fresh, completely original ideas in any art form are extremely rare. In a sense, the entire history of jazz could probably be summed up with three names: Armstrong, Hawkins, and Parker. But this would telescope the entire history of jazz to a dusty litany of unrelated "giants."

With the spate of reissues in recent years, precious 78's and even cylinders and piano rolls have been faithfully re-recorded on LP's which removes living moments of jazz history from archives and collections, making them available for the general public. Many apocryphal figures come to mind who could never be recorded and whose art remains a legend — Buddy Bolden, Porter King, Emmet Hardy, and Tony Jackson. Others like Freddie Keppard, Bunk Johnson, Alphonse Picou, and Larry Shields, who were recorded long after their prime, remain shadowy figures of a dim past. Still other tragic figures like Leon Rappalo, Joe Smith, Bix Beiderbecke, Hershal Evans, Fats Navarro, Clifford Brown, and Wardell Gray were stilled by permanent illness or untimely death.

Important contributors or consolidators like Henry "Red" Allen, Sidney Bechet, Charlie Shavers, Buck Clayton, Harry Edison, Lucky Thompson, Omer Simeon, Zoot Sims, Sonny Stitt, Jess Stacy, Bobby Hackett, Shorty Rogers, John Lewis, Frankie Newton, Joe Sullivan, and Mary Lou Williams have been excluded due to the exigencies of space. Although it is a truism that a creator is seldom if ever excelled by one of his disciples, the very term "creator" is open to question.

By definition a creator must transcend (Parker, Mole, Armstrong), consolidate (Peterson, Wilson, Noone), alter (Silver, Davis, Konitz), or even demolish (Powell, Young, Eldridge) previous levels of expression.

Each creator does not arbitrarily choose the role to be followed; rather this role is assigned by history. At the same time no creator alone can make his achievement; he is constantly aided by figures of probably less stature who often point the way toward a new imaginative level. From this point of view, the sum total of these minor figures is extremely important and refutes the myth of the solitary "cultural hero."

To assume that the best of jazz has been captured on records is, of course, ridiculous; and the painful remembrance which we all have felt of past, lost moments only points up the inescapable silence of history. Like any art form, jazz displays an inevitable dialectic toward more comprehensive modes of expression — but it is also well to keep in mind that any invidious comparisons in which one period (either the earliest or the latest) is chosen as an absolute of expression in distinction to another period, or all other periods, is to miss completely the intrinsic worth of every period. It must be remembered that each line chosen is a fair representation of the finest conception for that particular period, and in no way is to be deemed a series of progressive steps from bad to good or inept to skilled.

The obvious extension and refinement of skills and techniques must be thought of as representative of a comparable progressive extension of feeling and thinking on the part of the successive generation of people who listened to this music.

If a King Oliver chorus seems archaic and limited to a modern listener, it is well to remember that Charlie Parker would have appeared as incomprehensible emotionally and intellectually to the audiences at Chicago's Lincoln Gardens in 1923.

This is the natural evolution of any art form, and if the art form possesses an intrinsic worth, each period should retain some permanent value relative to all periods besides its absolute value to its own particular space-time. In other words, Armstrong's "Potato Head Blues" should and does possess a *universality* for all periods. This *universality* will probably never completely recapture the excitement of the moment of creation, but some permanent verity must always reside in Louis' achievement.

Here, then, is a book which permanently records the evolution of the improvised line and the history of jazz rhythm with the hope that future generations may find here knowledge to aid them in their efforts toward continuing and deepening the jazz art.

JOHN MEHEGAN

SECTION I

Jazz Rhythm

LESSON 1.

General

All jazz involves three levels of time (rhythmic pulsation) played simultaneously against each other. It is the constant conflict of these three time levels and their superimpositions which results in the endless tension present in jazz.

The idea of rhythmic "counterpoint" is, of course, present in all music (Western and Eastern), so that this fact alone would not account for the unique qualities associated with jazz. However, jazz deals almost exclusively with a *specific* relationship of time values which immediately distinguishes it from a large segment of other musical forms. This specific relationship of time values can best be expressed through their application to melody, harmony, and rhythm.

As a general statement, it can be said that all jazz from 1900 to the present day has employed the following ratio of time values:

1. A quarter-note pulse, the *rhythmic unit,* representing the rhythmic *center of gravity* of any jazz performance.

2. A *slower* set of time values representing the *harmonic unit* (half-note).

3. A *quicker* set of time values representing the *melodic unit* (eighth-note).

In Lesson 34 of Volume I, we learned that the melodic unit employs variables ranging from eighth-note to thirty-second-note. This range was incomplete and was established for study purposes. The following outline illustrates the variables for the three basic units which have been employed through the years from New Orleans polyphony to modern jazz.

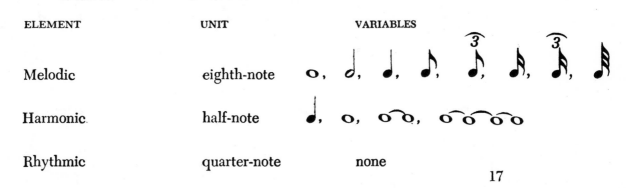

ELEMENT	UNIT	VARIABLES
Melodic	eighth-note	
Harmonic	half-note	
Rhythmic	quarter-note	none

17

In the above outline, dotted values are assumed to be included; syncopation will be discussed in a later lesson.

As we trace the history of jazz, we find that the rhythmic unit has seldom if ever varied through the course of some sixty years. We will also discover in this and succeeding lessons that the harmonic and melodic variables have gradually expanded through the years from the complex to the more complex.

It is also apparent that the rhythmic "assignments" for certain jazz instruments have drastically changed — some to the point of altering the role of the instrument from one level of time to another:

INSTRUMENT	BEFORE	NOW
Piano	rhythmic	harmonic
Bass	harmonic	rhythmic
Guitar	rhythmic	melodic and/or rhythmic
Drums	rhythmic	melodic and/or rhythmic

RHYTHMIC SUPERIMPOSITION

As the range of variables has increased on the melodic and harmonic levels, so also has the superimposition of these units and their variables, one level over another. The idea of rhythmic superimposition has always existed in jazz and can even be found in examples of archaic folk idioms.

For instance:

Fig. 1.

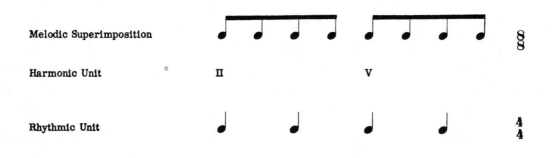

18

Fig. 2.

These functional superimpositions have existed in jazz and pre-jazz for probably 75 years. The first example is common to nearly all boogie-woogie; the second is common to archaic folk guitar and remains the rhythmic staple of rock and roll.

Sometimes the superimposed factor is the rhythmic unit (quarter-note), which may appear on either the melodic level (especially Armstrong and Beiderbecke) Fig. 3; or on the harmonic level (especially Tatum-Wilson swing bass) Fig. 4.

Fig. 3.

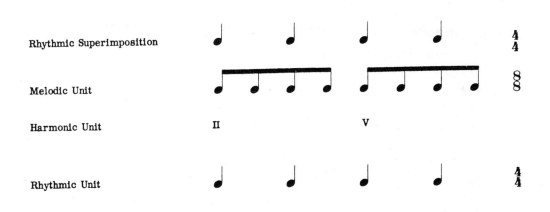

In Fig. 3 the rhythmic superimposition over the melodic unit was employed by Armstrong and Beiderbecke to build the rhythmic tension later to be released into the eighth-note melodic unit.

It is of course apparent that the major superimpositions in rhythmic units have been melodic over harmonic (Fig. 1 and 2) and in relation to the piano the gradual transition from a rhythmic to a harmonic and finally, a melodic instrument. Melodic over rhythmic has played a major role in the emergence of modern drumming (e.g. the drum solo). The necessary "static" value of the harmonic unit has resulted in few displacements to the other levels. Fig. 5 is a broad outline of the essential displacements of each level.

Fig. 4.

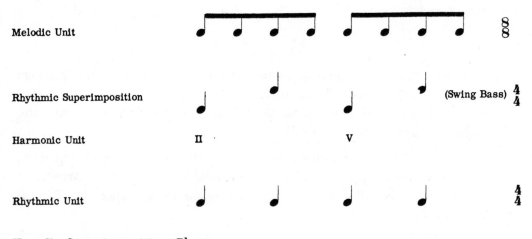

Fig. 5. Superimposition Chart

Melodic over harmonic:
  Boogie-woogie (Fig. 1)
  12/8 time (rock and roll) (Fig. 2)
  Modern solo piano
  Locked hands
  New Orleans clarinet obligato
  Left hand arpeggiation
  Banjo
Melodic over rhythmic:
  Wood block or cymbal
  Drum solo
Rhythmic over melodic:
  New Orleans — Chicago "ride out" (Fig. 3)
Rhythmic over harmonic:
  Guitar
  Ragtime
  Swing bass
  "Walking" bass lines
  Erroll Garner (left hand "strumming" in quarter-note units)

20

The device of superimposition of one level over another raises the question as to what is a melodic, harmonic, or rhythmic instrument. Although each instrument in a jazz group (except the drum) is concerned with harmonic materials, there actually is no such thing as a harmonic instrument in jazz (the exception might be the New Orleans trombone). In each case the harmonic materials are transformed into melodic or rhythmic elements. In essence, all factors ultimately emerge as rhythmic.

The following designations indicate the roles of the basic jazz instruments in the history of jazz:

New Orleans:
    Melodic: cornet (1)
    Melodic-Harmonic: clarinet
                    cornet (2)
                    banjo*
    Harmonic: trombone
    Rhythmic-Harmonic: piano
                    tuba-bass
    Rhythmic: drums

*The banjo represents a curious anomaly of factors: It is essentially a "harmonic" instrument ♩, it utilizes "melodic" units ♪♪, yet it is traditionally considered a component of the "rhythmic" section ♩

Chicago†:
    Melodic: trumpet
    Melodic-Harmonic: clarinet
                    saxophone
                    trombone
                    piano (R. H.)
    Rhythmic-Harmonic: piano (L. H.)
                    banjo-guitar
                    bass
    Rhythmic: drums

†The term "Chicago" refers to the small polyphonic ensembles existing from 1924 to 1932. The New York scene of the " '20's" is generally one of experimentation with resources destined to become the large ensemble structure of the " '30's." The unique development of the Ellington band is beyond the scope of this book.

Swing:
    Melodic: brass or reeds
    Melodic-Harmonic: brass or reeds
    Rhythmic-Harmonic: piano
                             guitar
                             bass
    Rhythmic: drums

Progressive:
    Melodic: saxophone-trumpet unison
    Melodic-Harmonic: piano
    Rhythmic-Harmonic: bass
    Rhythmic: drums

At no time should this material be interpreted as indicating a general progress from "bad" to "good" (as some believe) or "good" to "bad" (as others believe). Each style portrays emotions and feelings in context to its particular space-time. Armstrong's "West End Blues" is as valid as Parker's "Koko," and Beiderbecke's "Singin' the Blues" is comparable to either of the previously mentioned performances. Each represents a milestone of achievement in context to a particular period, style, and point of view.

SUMMARY: Jazz is an improvised indigenous American folk music employing eighth-, half-, and quarter-note rhythmic units moving through a diatonic system of harmony in 4/4 time.

LESSON 2.

Tempo

Tempo in jazz has always been a primary consideration for the performer in choosing the pulsation best suited for "swing" and urgency. However, tempo has often been affected by factors not directly connected with rhythm, such as individual virtuosity. A performer naturally chooses a tempo which will allow him to achieve his ideas with clarity and precision. In this case, a tempo might be considered "too slow" if the performer felt unable to create the necessary "ideas" to fill the large spatial areas created by a "slow" tempo. On the other hand, a tempo would probably be considered "too fast" if the performer's ability with the eighth-note unit, the *sine qua non,* were over-taxed.

Two other factors extraneous to the performer come into play in determining tempo:

1. Social function

2. Prevailing harmonic materials

Social functions such as the New Orleans funerals and weddings, also prevailing dance styles (Charleston, Lindy, etc.), may determine to a large extent the permissible tempo range.

Prevailing harmonic materials (the chord chart) also affect tempo. If a chord chart employs long sustained harmonic units (𝅝𝅝𝅝𝅝), a certain pulsation rate must be maintained in order to achieve any urgency. On the other hand, the use of quick harmonic units (𝅗𝅥 𝅗𝅥 | 𝅘𝅥 𝅘𝅥 𝅘𝅥 𝅘𝅥) would necessarily mean some moderation in tempo in order for the performer to "realize" each chord.

The following outline illustrates the history of tempo in jazz from the early Twenties to the present day. In each case the metronome marking (mm) refers to the rhythmic unit (quarter-note).

These estimates are based on arbitrary samplings and indicate only the general trends.

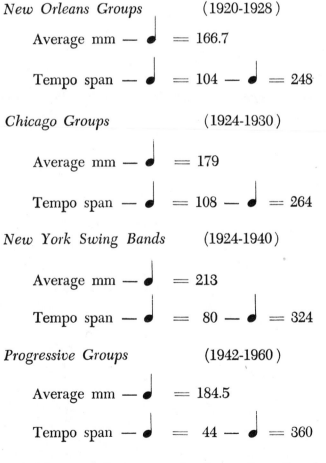

New Orleans Groups   (1920-1928)

    Average mm — ♩ = 166.7

    Tempo span — ♩ = 104 — ♩ = 248

Chicago Groups   (1924-1930)

    Average mm — ♩ = 179

    Tempo span — ♩ = 108 — ♩ = 264

New York Swing Bands   (1924-1940)

    Average mm — ♩ = 213

    Tempo span — ♩ = 80 — ♩ = 324

Progressive Groups   (1942-1960)

    Average mm — ♩ = 184.5

    Tempo span — ♩ = 44 — ♩ = 360

Many conclusions can be drawn from the above outline:

Tempo averages gradually increased until the Progressive period when a noticeable decline occurred. There were many reasons for this decline in the Forties.

    a) More complex harmonic materials

    b) Growing emphasis on mood and formal structure

    c) A probing of the "slow sound barrier" (below mm ♩ = 100) to hitherto unheard areas (mm ♩ = 44)

    d) General abandonment of the eighth-note as the sole improvising unit with an accompanying exploration of the sixteenth-note triplet and thirty-second-note at slower tempi; trend toward introspection

    e) The "fast sound barrier" (♩ = 300) has maintained to some extent, but the average drops because of the slow tempi. (Note: the fastest recorded solo known to the author is "Indiana" by Oscar Peterson (♩ = 360)

Contrary to popular opinion, Chicago jazz was not much faster than New Orleans jazz; the tradition from Chicago to Swing is much more accelerated. The tempo spans of the New Orleans and Chicago groups are fairly similar. The explanation of the "fast" Chicago myth may lie in the fact that the levels of musicianship in the Chicago groups were uneven and the slower efforts have not withstood the ravages of time, whereas the "enthusiastic" quicker tempi have survived. This dictum would of course exclude Beiderbecke, Trumbauer, Lang, and "Miff" Mole.

It is doubtful if the modern tempo span of ♩ = 44-360 can be broadened. Below mm ♩ = 44, "swing" becomes questionable; above mm ♩ = 360 would seem to tax human limitation and probably also the possibilities of "swing."

Melodic Time Values

As previously indicated, the melodic instruments (trumpet, clarinet, saxophone) have from the beginning enjoyed the most freedom in terms of rhythmic units (eighth-note — thirty-second-note).

The following outline illustrates the over-all development of the melodic time unit in the improvised line:

	UNIT RANGE		
Bessie Smith	𝅝 (whole note)	to	♪ (eighth note)
"King" Oliver	𝅝 (whole note)	to	♩ (triplet quarter, marked 3)
Louis Armstrong	𝅗𝅥 (half note)	to	♪ (eighth note)
Roy Eldridge / Benny Goodman	♩ (quarter note)	to	♪ (eighth note)
Charlie Parker / Dizzy Gillespie	♩ (quarter note)	to	♬ (sixteenth/thirty-second note)

This outline reveals the gradual abandonment of the "vocal" line improvisation in favor of the "instrumental" line. The quarter-note unit appearing in each unit range represents the superimposition of the rhythmic over the melodic (see Fig. 3, Lesson 1).

Fig. 1 illustrates a schematic outline of the improvised line from Bessie Smith to Hampton Hawes, employing the eternal 12-bar blues. It will be noted that several of the soloists (especially Young and Davis) indicate a reaction against the generally expanding levels of virtuosity. These solos represent an interpretive attempt to explore new levels of harmonic and melodic insight, areas of equal importance. The varying signatures are all applicable to the figured bass appearing at the bottom.

27

28

34

POLYPHONY

In jazz, the term polyphony usually refers to the superimposing (see Lesson 1) of the melodic unit over the harmonic unit to form a *counter-melody, obligato,* or *ornamentation* to the melodic voices or melody. The classic prototype of this device is, of course, the clarinet obligato found in the New Orleans ensembles:

--------------------------------------Cornet 1

-------------------------------Cornet 2 (*obligato*)

-----------------------------Clarinet obligato

In general, the *superimposed melodic unit* in New Orleans polyphony is of a quicker value than the prevailing melodic unit. This would be true of both the cornet 2 obligato and the clarinet obligato.

CHICAGO POLYPHONY

Chicago polyphony is more florid than its New Orleans antecedent and is usually held up to question for its disorderly ebullience. This is a judgment beyond the scope of this text, although it should be noted that the rampant individualism of the Chicago ensembles was an inevitable result of the expanding concepts of melody, harmony, and rhythm. Also, it should be remembered that the art form had to move toward more personal areas of expression and eventually escape from the prison of New Orleans formalism. Armstrong himself, in the "Hot Five" and "Hot Seven" recordings, was a leading figure in this movement.

The appearance of the snare drum in both categories is to account for the quicker values (press-rolls, etc.) and the rhythmic pulse of quarter-notes. The accented quarter-notes on beats 2 and 4 will be treated in the section dealing with syncopation.

CHICAGO

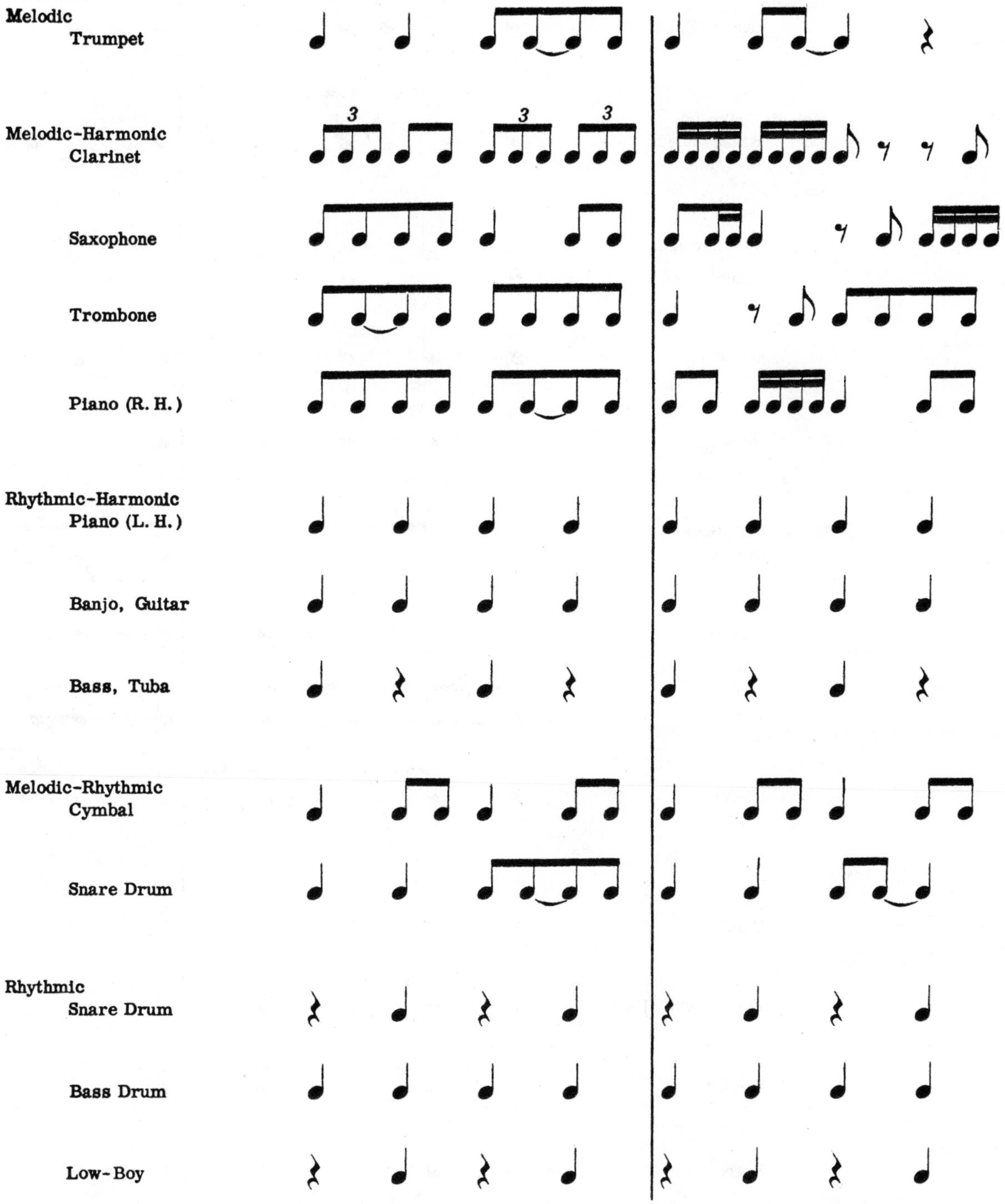
Melodic
Trumpet
Melodic-Harmonic
Clarinet
Saxophone
Trombone
Piano (R. H.)
Rhythmic-Harmonic
Piano (L. H.)
Banjo, Guitar
Bass, Tuba
Melodic-Rhythmic
Cymbal
Snare Drum
Rhythmic
Snare Drum
Bass Drum
Low-Boy

Melodic
    Brass, Reeds

Melodic-Harmonic
    Brass, Reeds
    (riffs)

Rhythmic-Harmonic
    Piano

    Guitar

    Bass

Melodic-Rhythmic
    Cymbal

    Snare

    Tom-Tom

    Hi-Hat

Rhythmic
    Cymbal

    Bass Drum

    Hi-Hat

    Snare Drum

       The appearance of the Hi-Hat cymbal in both categories refers to the similarly dual role of the snare drum.

PROGRESSIVE

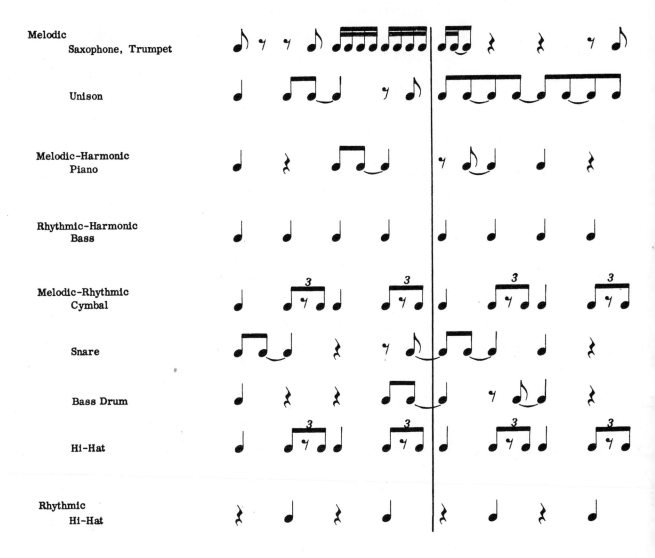

The major developments indicated by this outline are as follows:

NEW ORLEANS TO CHICAGO:

1. The abandonment by the trombone of the only pure harmonic role in jazz and its emergence as a melodic-harmonic instrument.

2. The introduction of the saxophone as a major jazz instrument.

3. The emergence of the piano as a major melodic-harmonic instrument.

4. Abandonment of the wood-block; introduction of both the "ride" cymbal and the Low-Boy cymbal.

5. Partial abandonment of group polyphony and emergence of the *hero*-improvisor.

CHICAGO TO SWING

1. Development of brass and reed sections playing in ensemble.

2. Quarter-note unit adopted by bass (Wellman Braud).

3. Introduction of the Hi-Hat cymbal.

4. Introduction of the melodic-rhythmic figure on the "ride" cymbal and the Hi-Hat cymbal.

5. Abandonment of the banjo; introduction of the guitar.

6. Introduction of accented 2 and 4 beats on Hi-Hat cymbal and "ride" cymbal.

SWING TO PROGRESSIVE

1. Return to small-group polyphony with homophonic (unison) innovations.

2. Development of melodic-harmonic role of the piano.

3. Emergence of the bass as the sole rhythmic instrument. Appearance of the bass as an important solo instrument.

4. Melodic-rhythmic innovations of drums which ceased to be the primary rhythmic instrument.

LESSON 4.

Harmonic Time Values

The history of jazz harmony concerns the dynamic changes effected on three levels:

1. The rhythmic procession of the chord qualities.

2. The expanding quality system joined with an equivalent expanding chromaticism.

3. The gradual abandonment of an inversion system based on the triad in favor of a root-position seventh-chord concept.

The following bass lines are representative charts of the New Orleans, Chicago, Swing, and Progressive periods. T indicates a triad (root, third, fifth.)

NEW ORLEANS

"Dippermouth Blues"

I^T / IVx / I^T / Ix / IVx / IVx / I^T / I^T / V / V / I^T / I^T //

DIPPERMOUTH BLUES —
  Used by permission of the copyright owner
  INTERNATIONAL MUSIC, INC., 745 Fifth Avenue, New York City.

"Milenburg Joys"

I^T / I^T / I^T / I^T / I^T / I^T / $V^{\frac{4}{3}}$ / $V^{\frac{4}{3}}$ / $V^{\frac{4}{3}}$ / $V^{\frac{4}{3}}$ / $V^{\frac{4}{3}}$ /

$V^{\frac{4}{3}}$ / $V^{\frac{4}{3}}$ / $V^{\frac{4}{3}}$ / I^T / I^T / I^T / I^T / I^T / I^T / Ix / Ix /

IV^T / IV^T / IV^T / $\sharp IVo$ / VI_2 / VIx / IIx / V / I^T / I^T //

MILENBERG JOYS — by Walter Melrose, Leon Roppolo, Paul Mares, "Jelly Roll" Morton
  Melrose Music Corp.
  Used by permission.

"Mandy Lee Blues"

VIx / VIx / IIx / IIx / V / V / I^T / I^T / VIx / VIx / IIx /

IIx / $\flat VIx$ / VI_2 VIx / IIx V / I VIx / IIx V / I^T //

MANDY LEE BLUES — by Walter Melrose & Morty Bloom
  Melrose Music Corp.
  Used by permission.

"High Society"

I^T / I^T / I^T / I^T / I^T / I^T / I^T / I^T $VI^{\frac{4}{3}}$ $\flat IIIo$ / $V^{\frac{4}{3}}$ /

V / I^T / I^T / III_2 / IIx / V / V / I^T / I^T / I^T / I^T / I^T /

I^T / I^T / I^T / IV^T / IVx / I^T / VIx / IIx / V / I^T / I^T /

I^T / I^T //

HIGH SOCIETY —
  Used by permission of the copyright owner
  INTERNATIONAL MUSIC, INC., 745 Fifth Avenue, New York City.

CHICAGO

"Singing The Blues"

pick-up

$\sharp$Io // II / V / I$^{+\,6}$ V / I$^{+\,6}$ $\sharp$Io / II / V / I$^{+\,6}$ / I$^{+\,6}$ / IIIx /

IIIx / VIx / VIx / IIx / VI IIx / V / V / II / V / I$^{+\,6}$ / I$^{+\,6}$ /

$\sharp$Io VIx / III VIx / II VIx$^{\,4}_{\,3}$ / II / IV$^{+\,6}$ / $\sharp$IVo / III / VIx /

IIx / V / I$^{+\,6}$ / I$^{+\,6}$ //

SINGIN' THE BLUES TILL MY DADDY COMES HOME —
   Copyright 1920 by Mills Music, Inc.
   Used by permission.

"Sweet Sue"

pick-up

III $\flat$IIIo // II IIϕ_2 / V$^6_5$ V / II IIϕ_2 / V$^6_5$ VII$_2$ / I$^{+\,6}$ / I$^{+\,6}$ /

I$^{+\,6}$ / I$^{+\,6}$ III $\flat$III / II IIϕ_2 / V$^6_5$ V / II IIϕ_2 / V$^6_5$ V / I$^{+\,6}$ /

I$^{+\,6}$ / I$^{+\,6}$ / I$^{+\,6}$ / I$^{+\,6}$ / III / III$\phi^{\,4}_{\,3}$ / VIx / II / II / IIϕ /

V III $\flat$III / II IIϕ_2 / V$^6_5$ V / II IIϕ_2 / V$^6_5$ V / I$^{+\,6}$ / IVx /

I$^{+\,6}$ / I$^{+\,6}$ //

SWEET SUE — JUST YOU — Words by Will J. Harris, Music by Victor Young
   COPYRIGHT MCMXXVIII by Shapiro, Bernstein & Co. Inc.
   Copyright Renewed MCMLV and Assigned to Shapiro, Bernstein & Co. Inc.
   Used by permission of Shapiro, Bernstein & Co. Inc., 666 Fifth Avenue, New York 19, N. Y.

"I Wish I Could Shimmy Like My Sister Kate"

V$^{\,4}_{\,3}$ V / V$^{\,4}_{\,3}$ V / I$^{+\,6}$ VI$_2$ / I$^{+\,6}$ $\sharp$Io / V$^{\,4}_{\,3}$ V / V$^{\,4}_{\,3}$ V / I$^{+\,6}$ /

I$^{+\,6}$ $\sharp$Io / V$^{\,4}_{\,3}$ V / V$^{\,4}_{\,3}$ V / I$^{+\,6}$ / Ix / IV$^{+\,6}$ $\sharp$IVo / VI$_2$ VIx /

IIx V / I$^{+\,6}$ VIx / IIx V / I$^{+\,6}$ //

I WISH I COULD SHIMMY LIKE MY SISTER KATE — Armand J. Piron
   Used by special permission of copyright owner Jerry Vogel
   Music Company, Inc., New York 36, N. Y.

"Jazz Me Blues"

(Verse) I^{+6} VI_2 / I^{+6} VI_2 / I VIx / IIx V / I^{+6} I_2 / VI VI_2 /

$\flat$Vo / V I^{+6} / I^{+6} VI_2 / I^{+6} VI_2 / I VI / IIx V / I^{+6} I_2 /

VI VI_2 / $\flat$Vo / V I^{+6} // (Break) V / Vo / V / V //

(Chorus) VIx / VIx / IIx / IIx / V / V / I^{+6} / I^{+6} / VIx /

VIx / IIx / IIx / I^{+6} / $IIIx^{\frac{4}{3}}$ / VI / VIx / IIx / V / I^{+6} / I^{+6} //

SWING

"Oh, Lady Be Good"

I $Ix^{\frac{4}{3}}$ / IVx / I / $\sharp$Io / II / V / I^{+6} VI / II V / I $Ix^{\frac{4}{3}}$ / IVx /

I / $\sharp$Io / II / V / I^{+6} / Ix / IV^{+6} / $\sharp$IVo / VI_2 / I / VI /

IIx / II / V / I $Ix^{\frac{4}{3}}$ / IVx / I / $\sharp$Io / II / V / I^{+6} / I^{+6} //

"Just You, Just Me"

I^{+6} $III\phi^{\frac{4}{3}}$ / VIx / II / V / Ix / IV^{+6} IVm^{+6} / VI_2 V /

I^{+6} / I^{+6} $III\phi^{\frac{4}{3}}$ / VIx / II / V / Ix / IV^{+6} IVm^{+6} / VI_2 V /

I^{+6} / Ix / Ix / IV^{+6} / $\flat$VIIx / I^{+6} / $IIIx^{\frac{4}{3}}$ VI / IIx / V /

I $III\phi^{\frac{4}{3}}$ / VIx / II / V / Ix / IV^{+6} IVm^{+6} / VI_2 V / I^{+6} //

"Tea For Two"

(A♭) II V / II V / I VI$_2$ / I$^6_5$ ♭IIIo / II V / II V / I / I //

(C) II V / II V / I VI$_2$ / I$^6_5$ ♭IIIo / II V / II V / I^{+6} //

(A♭) V / II V / II V / I VI$_2$ / I$^6_5$ ♭IIIo / II V / II V / IIIφ /

(A♭) VIx / II ♭IIo / II VIx / ♯Io II / ♭Vφ IVm^{+6} / VI$^4_3$ ♭IIIo /

(A♭) II V / I^{+6} / I^{+6} //

"Whispering"

I^{+6} / I^{+6} / ♭Vm / VIIx / I^{+6} / I^{+6} / ♭VIIx. / VIx / IIx /

IIx / V / V / I^{+6} / III ♭IIIo / II / V / I^{+6} / I^{+6} / ♭Vm /

VIIx / I^{+6} / I^{+6} / ♭VIIx / VIx / IIx / IIx / V / V / II /

V$^{♯3}$ / I^{+6} / I^{+6} //

PROGRESSIVE

"I Can't Get Started"

(C) I VI / II V / VIIm IIIx ♭VIIm ♭IIIx / VI IIx ♭VI ♭IIx /

(C) I VI / II V$^{♯3}$ / IIIx$^{♭5}$ VIx$^{♭5}$ / IIx$^{♭5}$ V$^{♭5}$ / I VI / II V /

(C) VIIm IIIx ♭VIIm ♭IIIx / VI IIx ♭VI ♭IIx / I VI / II V$^{♯3}$ /

(C) I^{+6} ♯I / I^{+6} I // (D) II V / ♭Vφ IVo / III II / I I^{+6} //

(C) II V / ♭Vφ IVo / III ♭IIIx / IIx ♭IIx / I VI / II V /

(C) VIIm IIIx ♭VIIm ♭IIIx / VI IIx ♭VI ♭IIx / I VI / II V$^{♯3}$ //

(C) (Coda) IIIφ / VIx$^{♭5}$ / IIφ / V$^{♭5}$ / I$^{♭5}$ / I$^{♭5}$ //

"Night In Tunisia"

(c) ♭IIx / I / ♭IIx / I / ♭IIx / I VI / II ♭IIx / I^{+6} / ♭IIx /

(c) I / ♭IIx / I / ♭IIx / I VI / II ♭IIx / I^{+6} // (f) II / V /

(f) I^{+6} ♭IIx / I^{+6} // (E♭) II / V / I IV // (c) II V /

(c) ♭IIx / I / ♭IIx / I / ♭IIx / I VI / II ♭IIx / I^{+6} //

(c) (interlude) II / II / ♭IIx / ♭IIx / I / Im / IVx$^{♭5}$ / IVx$^{♭5}$ //

(E♭) VIx$^{♭5}$ / VIx$^{♭5}$/ IIIx / IIIx // (break) I / I / I / I // *note

*note — break may be optional two or four bars.

NIGHT IN TUNISIA — by Frank Paparelli, John "Dizzy" Gillespie
   Copyright MCMXLIV by LEEDS MUSIC CORPORATION, 322 West 48th Street,
   New York 36, N. Y.
   Used by permission. All rights reserved.

"Lady Bird"

(C) I / VI / IVm / ♭VIIx / I / VI // (A♭) II / V / I / I //

(C) VI / IIx / II / IVo / III ♭IIIx / II ♭IIx / I / VI / IVm /

(C) ♭VIIx / I / VI // (A♭) II / V / I / I // (C) VI / IIx /

(C) II / ♭IIx / I^{+6} / I^{+6} //

LADY BIRD (HALF NELSON) —
   Used by permission of Savoy Music Company, Newark, New Jersey.

"Bernie's Tune"

(d) I / I / IIIm / ♭VIx / II / V / I^{+6} / I^{+6} / I / I / IIIm /

(d) ♭VIx / II / V / I^{+6} / I^{+6} // (B♭) I^{+6} VI / II ♭IIx /

(B♭) I^{+6} VI / II ♭IIx / I^{+6} VI / II ♭IIx / I^{+6} VI // (d) II ♭IIx /

(d) I / I / IIIm / ♭VIx / II / V / I^{+6} / I^{+6} //

BERNIE'S TUNE —
   Copyright 1953-1954-1955 by ATLANTIC MUSIC CORP., by arrangement with SKY VIEW
   MUSIC CORP. Sole Selling Agent: CRITERION MUSIC CORP., R.K.O. Bldg., Radio City,
   New York 20, N. Y.
   International Copyright Secured. Used by permission.

THE NEW ORLEANS-CHICAGO TRANSITION

1. Abandonment of the triadic system in favor of seventh chord concepts. This meant a transition from a harmonic system composed of the following factors: to one composed of:

major triad	major added sixth chord
minor triad	dominant seventh
diminished triad	minor seventh
dominant seventh	diminished seventh

The half-diminished chord appeared for the first time in this transition but was sparingly employed only in the second inversion.

2. A strong development toward the use of inversions can be explained by an emerging modal scale and arpeggio concept increasingly employed by tuba and bass players.

3. A general abandonment of the basic 𝅝 𝅝 New Orleans harmonic unit in favor of the basic 𝅝 Chicago harmonic unit in addition to the occasional use of the emerging 𝅗𝅥 harmonic unit.

4. Abandonment of the IIx (the New Orleans preparation for V) in favor of the natural diatonic II (minor).

5. Chicago use of III and IIIx usually not present in New Orleans style.

6. Some expanding use of keys. The C, G, F, B♭, E♭ spectrum of New Orleans jazz was extended to A♭, D♭, and D in the Chicago period.

THE CHICAGO-SWING TRANSITION

1. The emergence of chromatic harmony in the extended use of such non-diatonic factors as ♭VIIx, ♭Vm, ♭Vφ, ♭IIIx.

2. Partial disappearance of the x $\frac{4}{3}$ inversion. All root position dominants prepared by the minor or half-diminished chord a perfect fifth above. Initial use of the $\frac{6}{5}$ inversion.

3. Initial appearance of the major seventh chord and the root-position half-diminished chord — the final emergence of the sixty chord system.

4. Appearance of modulation in the jazz bass line.

5. Elementary twelve key facility.

6. Consolidation of the 𝅝, 𝅗𝅥 harmonic unit.

7. Appearance of the professional songwriter, a specialized craftsman challenging the performing clichés of the jazz musician.

THE SWING-PROGRESSIVE TRANSITION

1. Appearance of advanced twelve key facility.

2. Further exploration of the 𝅗𝅥 unit at tempos exceeding mm—200.

3. Initial exploration of the minor scale-tone seventh chords (see Lesson 65, Volume I).

4. Full development of the half-diminished (*the sensual seventh*) chord (see Lesson 4).

5. Total disappearance of the triadic inversion accompanied by a general adoption of the circle of fifths.

6. Appearance of ♭IIx (modern variant of the Neapolitan Sixth) as a substitute chord for V.

7. Expanding *vertical* concepts of harmony utilizing polytonal structures.

8. Exploration of the 𝅘𝅥 harmonic unit.

Post-bop explorations of non-diatonic and asymmetrical resources have not in general been consolidated into any permanent achievement justifying inclusion here. This is not to dismiss these endeavors, but simply to state a general position of this text to deal only with enduring diatonic developments conceived in 4/4 time.

LESSON 5.

Syncopation

Jazz syncopation may be sub-divided into the following categories:

1. Simple syncopation involving accent only.

2. Compound syncopation involving notation (tied notes and rest values) and accent.

3. Multiple syncopation involving two or more levels of syncopation played simultaneously.

Applied to our three units of time () we derive the following:

SIMPLE RHYTHMIC SYNCOPATION

The quarter-note is the basic rhythmic unit. A bar of quarter-notes may be sub-divided into the following sub-units:

down beat	up beat	down beat	up beat

The syncopated unit here is the UP BEAT ACCENT (Fig. 1), the hallmark of all jazz; the universal catalyst identifying this music in all its rhythmic, sensual, ethnic, and psychological implications. This syncopation has at times been implied (New Orleans), explicit (Chicago, Swing), or concealed (Progressive), but its presence has never and probably, as long as there is jazz, will never decline. Its essence is quite simple — the constant interruption of the eternal symmetry of *one*, the *beginning* of melody, harmony, and rhythm.

Fig. 1.

foot beat

SIMPLE HARMONIC SYNCOPATION:

Syncopation of this unit occurs only in cases of melodic or rhythmic superimposition (see Lesson 1). Without superimposition, the harmonic unit cannot be syncopated.

SIMPLE MELODIC SYNCOPATION:

The eighth-note is the basic melodic unit. A bar of eighth-notes may be sub-divided into the following sub-units:

on beat	off beat	on beat	off beat	on beat	off beat	on beat	off beat

The syncopated unit here is the *off-beat accent* (Fig. 2) (see Lesson 58, Vol. I). The off-beat accents represent the syncopation of the *melodic* unit as the up-beat represent the syncopation of the *rhythmic* unit. The off-beat accent in a sense interrupts the up-beat accent which in itself is an interruption of the basic pulse (Fig. 3). The joining of these two levels of syncopation creates a pleasurable tension often referred to as the *swing* of a jazz performance.

Fig. 2.

foot beat

Fig. 3.

COMPOUND SYNCOPATION:

Simple syncopation occurs either on the *rhythmic* (♩) or the *melodic* (♪) levels; compound syncopation occurs only on the *melodic* level and involves either the use of the tie, or the rest, or both. It may involve the ♪ unit or any of its *variables*. Fig. 4 illustrates examples of compound syncopation common to any jazz performance (see schematic outline, Lesson 3).

Fig. 4.

foot beat

foot beat

50

foot beat

MULTIPLE SYNCOPATION:

On the actual performing level, only the drummer or the pianist in a jazz group is able to execute multiple syncopation. Skill in this area is essential to any jazz instrumentalist; first, in order to execute one syncopation level while one or more levels are being simultaneously played by other members of the group; and secondly, in order to *pre-hear* one syncopation (to be played in the succeeding bar) while actually playing another. The basic device in this area (aside from pre-hearing rhythmic shifts, e.g., eighth to sixteenth to thirty-second, etc.) is one of maintaining the prevailing rhythmic unit while alternating between *duple* and *triple* accents.

1. Duple (division of 2)

2. Triple (division of 3)

However, by the use of syncopation, it is possible to create a series of hybrid rhythms, which result in the following combinations:

EXTERNAL PULSE	INTERNAL ACCENT
duple	division of 3
triple	division of 2

This is a familiar device employed by all jazz musicians. The accented sub-divisions of the eighth-note and the sixteenth-note are the usual areas of this technique. The thirty-second-note is usually treated as an uninterrupted florid design to effect a contrast with the interrupted eighth- and sixteenth-note.

51

TRIPLE 8/8 TIME

Fig. 5 illustrates a normal duple procession of eighth-notes. Fig. 6 illustrates these tones played with an *internal accent of three*. This design is most effective when the accented tone appears *above* the two unaccented tones (Fig. 7).

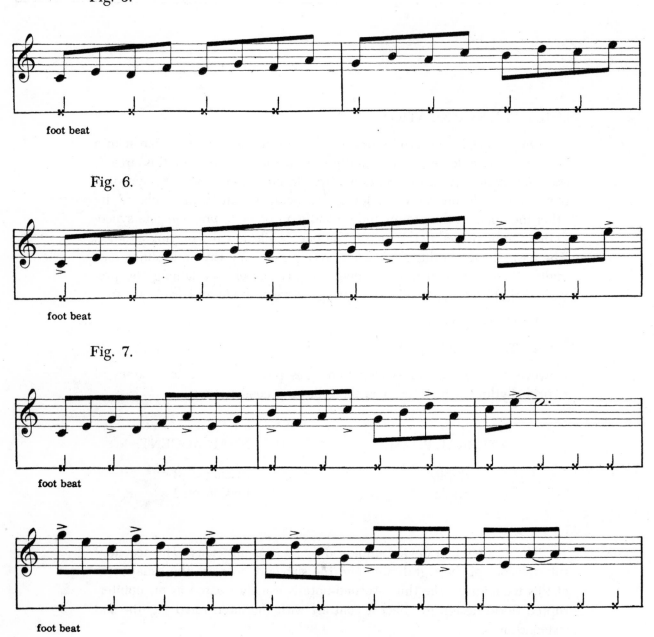

Fig. 5.

foot beat

Fig. 6.

foot beat

Fig. 7.

foot beat

foot beat

DUPLE 12/8 TIME

Fig. 8 illustrates the normal appearance of a bar of 12/8 time. Fig. 9 illustrates the same bar when played with an *internal accent of two*.

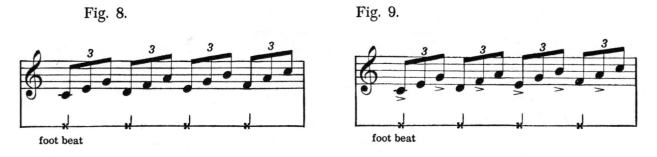

Fig. 8.

Fig. 9.

foot beat

foot beat

TRIPLE 6/16 TIME

Fig. 10 illustrates the normal appearance of a group of six-sixteenth-notes in a 4/4 pulse. This unit may be played in a number of ways:

1. With an internal accent on tones 1 and 4 (Fig. 11).

2. With an internal accent on tones 1, 3, and 5 (Fig. 12).

3. With an internal accent on tones 2, 4, and 6 (Fig. 13).

4. With an internal accent on tones 1 and 5 (Fig. 14).

5. With an internal accent on tones 3 and 6 (Fig. 15).

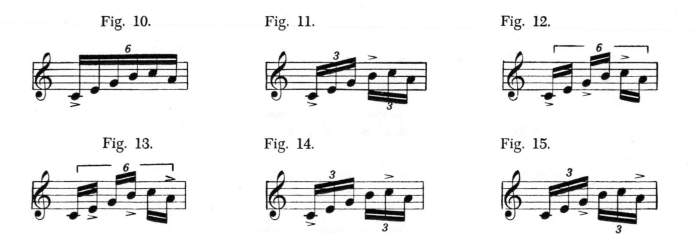

Fig. 10.

Fig. 11.

Fig. 12.

Fig. 13.

Fig. 14.

Fig. 15.

DRILL: The following rhythm series is to be practiced on any flat surface for developing facility in superimposing *internal* accents over *external* pulses:

7. R. H.

L. H.

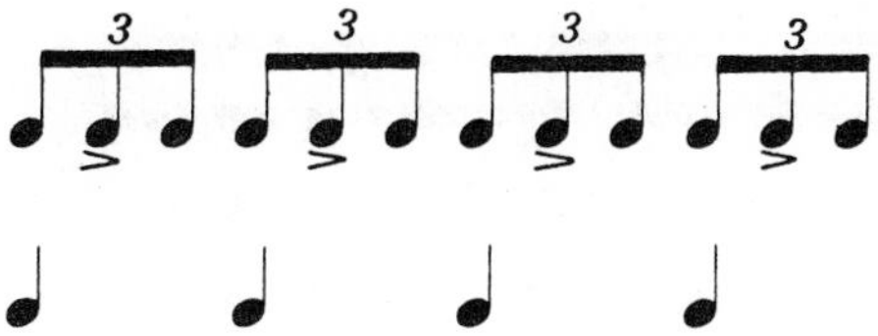

8. R. H.

L. H.

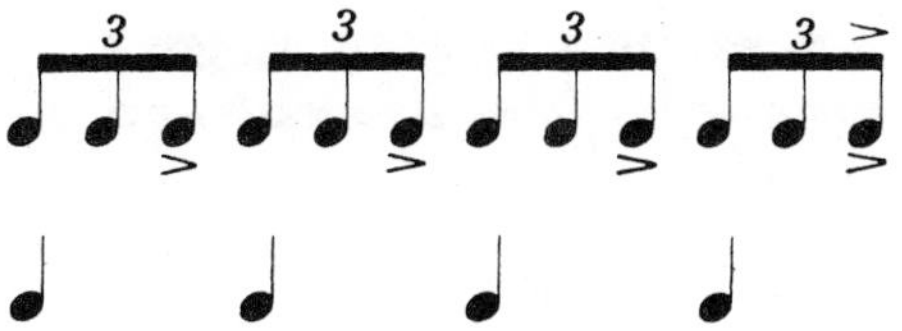

9. R. H.

L. H.

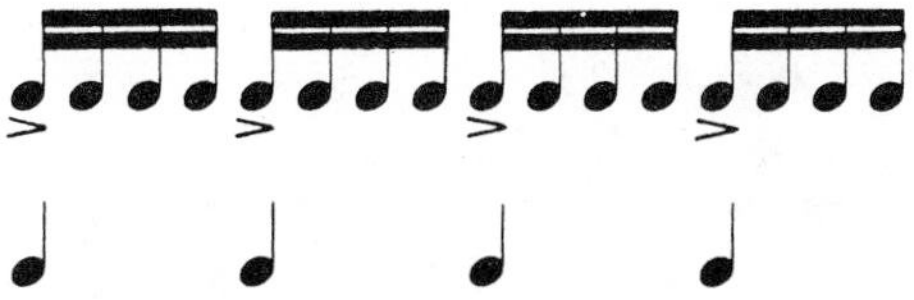

10. R. H.

L. H.

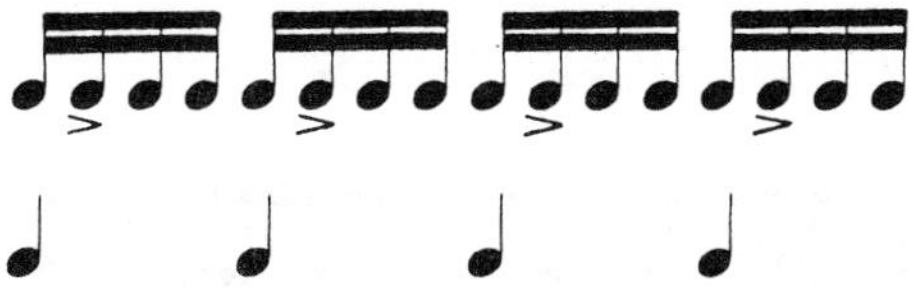

11. R. H.

L. H.

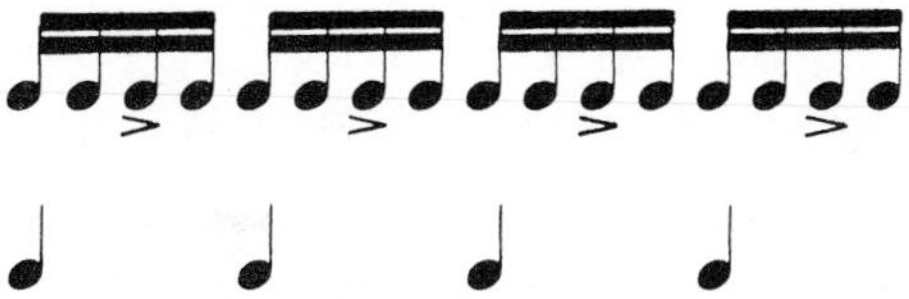

12. R. H.

L. H.

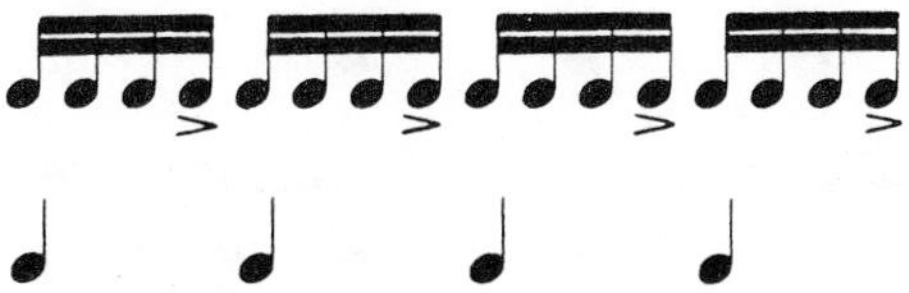

13. R. H.

L. H.

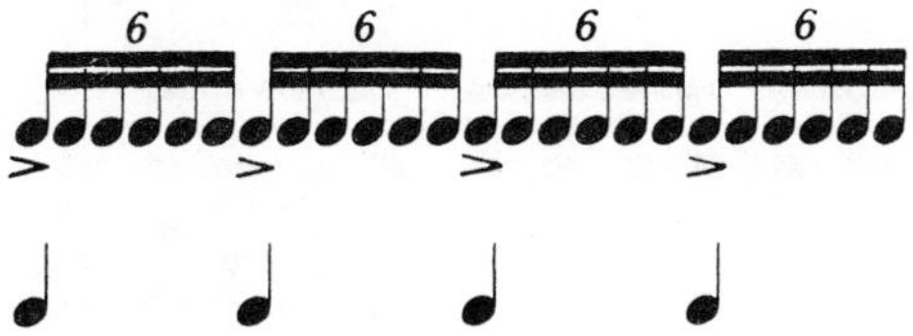

56

57

58

SECTION II

The improvised line (1923-1958)

NEW ORLEANS

"Gin House Blues":
Bessie Smith
Columbia CL 1036
Troy-Henderson
"High Society":
Johnny Dodds
Folkways FP 57
Joe Oliver
"Dippermouth Blues":
Joe Oliver
Riverside RLP 12-122
Armstrong-Oliver

"West End Blues":
Louis Armstrong
Columbia CL 853
Joe Oliver
"Muggles":
Louis Armstrong
Columbia CL 853
Armstrong-Hines
"Basin Street Blues":
Louis Armstrong
Columbia CL 852
Spencer Williams

CHICAGO

"Sweet Sue":
Bix Beiderbecke
Columbia CL 509
Victor Young
"Singin' The Blues":
Bix Beiderbecke
Columbia CL 845
Robinson-Conrad
"Original Dixieland One Step":
Miff Mole
Folkways FP 67
Nick LaRocca

"There'll Be Some Changes Made":
Frank Teschemacher
Folkways FP 65
Overstreet
"I'm Comin' Virginia":
Bix Beiderbecke
Columbia CL 845
Heywood-Cook
"Jazz Me Blues":
Bix Beiderbecke
Folkways FP 65
T. Delaney

SWING

"After You've Gone":
Roy Eldridge
Okeh 6278
Klenner

"Soft Winds"
(blues in A♭):
Benny Goodman
Columbia CL 1036
Benny Goodman

SWING (cont'd)

"Sweet Sue":
    Teddy Wilson
    Victor LPM 1226
    Victor Young
"Aunt Hager's Blues":
    Art Tatum
    Capitol T 216
    W. C. Handy

"Crazy Rhythm":
    Benny Carter-Coleman Hawkins
    Victor EP 447-0167
    Meyer and Kahn

EARLY PROGRESSIVE

"Just You, Just Me":
    Lester Young
    Keynote 603B
    J. Greer
"I Can't Get Started":
    Dizzy Gillespie
    Columbia CL 1036
    Ira Gershwin, Vernon Duke
"Half-Nelson"
  ("Lady Bird"):
    Miles Davis
    Savoy MG 12009
    "Tadd" Dameron

"Nice Work If You Can Get It":
    Bud Powell
    Roost RLP 401
    George Gershwin
"Koko" ("Cherokee"):
    Charlie Parker
    Savoy 12079
    Ray Noble
"Just Friends":
    Charlie Parker
    Clet 675
    Lewis-Klenner

LATE PROGRESSIVE

"Lover Man":
    Lee Konitz
    Pacific Jazz LP-2
    Davis-Ramirez-Sherman
"All The Things You Are":
    Chet Baker
    Pacific Jazz PJ 1206
    Jerome Kern
"Wrap Your Troubles In Dreams":
    Stan Getz
    New Jazz 8214
    Barris-Koehler-Moll

"Ghost Of A Chance":
    Clifford Brown
    Emarcy MG 36008
    Crosby-Washington-Young
"Opus De Funk":
    Horace Silver
    Blue Note 1520
    Horace Silver
"I've Got The World On A String":
    Oscar Peterson
    Verve 8268
    Harold Arlen

New Orleans

GIN HOUSE BLUES   BESSIE SMITH

HIGH SOCIETY

JOHNNY DODDS

DIPPERMOUTH BLUES

JOE OLIVER

WEST END BLUES

LOUIS ARMSTRONG

Ad lib. Intro

V+   Tempo   I+6   I+6

I+6   Ix   IV+6

IV+6   IVm+6   I+6

WEST END BLUES — by Clarence Wiliams, Joe Oliver
© Copyright MCMXXVIII by PICKWICK MUSIC CORPORATION
22 West 48th Street, New York 36, N. Y.
322 West 48th Street, New York 36, N. Y.

I+6   V

V   I+6

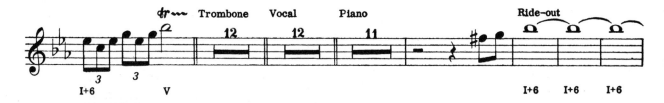

I+6   V   I+6   I+6   I+6

Ix   IV+6

IV+6   5

I+6   I+6

IVm+6   I+6   IVm   I+6

65

MUGGLES

LOUIS ARMSTRONG

Break (Double time)

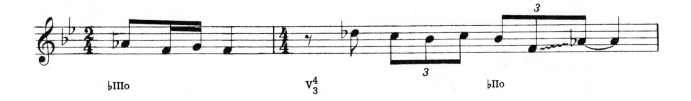

♭IIIo V_3^4 ♭IIo

V_3^4 V+   I+6   Ix   Io   IIø2

I+6   V   I+6   IIx   V

I+6   Ix   IVx

IVx   IVm+6   I+6   I+6 VI_3^4 ♭IIIo

V_3^4 V II_3^4 ♯VIo V_5^6 V

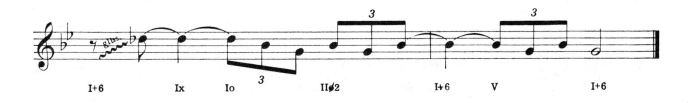

I+6   Ix   Io   IIø2   I+6   V   I+6

BASIN STREET BLUES

LOUIS ARMSTRONG

BASIN STREET BLUES — Words & Music — Spencer Williams Mayfair Music Corp.
Used by permission.

PART 2
Chicago

SWEET SUE — JUST YOU

BIX BEIDERBECKE

SINGIN' THE BLUES TILL MY DADDY COMES HOME

BIX BEIDERBECKE

pick-up

#Io   II   V#5   I+6   V

I+6   #Io   II   V   I+6

I+6   IIIx   IIIx   VIx   VIx

IIx   VI   IIx   V   V

II   V   I+6   V

I+6   #Io   VIx   III   VIx   II   VIx$^4_3$

II   II   #IIo   III

VIx   IIx   V   I+6   I+6

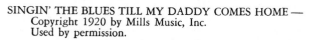

ORIGINAL DIXIELAND ONE-STEP

MIFF MOLE

I+6   Break   I+6   I+6

I+6   IIIx   IIIx   VIx

VIx   IIx   IIx   V

V   I+6   I+6   VIIx   VIIx

III   ♭IIIo   II   V   I+6   I+6

IIIx   IIIx   VIx   VIx

IIx   IIx   IV+6   IV+6   I+6

VIx   IIx   V   I+6   I+6

71

THERE'LL BE SOME CHANGES MADE

FRANK TESCHEMACHER

VIx   VIx   VIx

IIx   IIx   IIx

IIx   IIIx   IIIx

VIx   VIx   IIx

V   I+6   VIx

IIx   V   I+6   I+6

I'M COMING VIRGINIA

BIX BEIDERBECKE

I'M COMING VIRGINIA — Words by Will Marion Cook — Music by Donald Heywood

I+6   I+6   VIx   IIx

V   Ix   IV   IIIx ♭IIIx IIx   V

I+6   VI   II   V   I+6

I+6   III+6   III+6

♭V∅$\frac{4}{3}$ VIIx   III∅$\frac{4}{3}$ VIx   II∅$\frac{4}{3}$ V

Ix   IV+6   IV+6

II   V   II   V

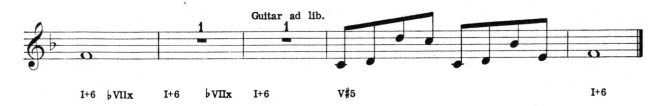

I+6 ♭VIIx   I+6   ♭VIIx   I+6   V#5   I+6

JAZZ ME BLUES

BIX BEIDERBECKE

PART 3
Swing

AFTER YOU'VE GONE

ROY ELDRIDGE

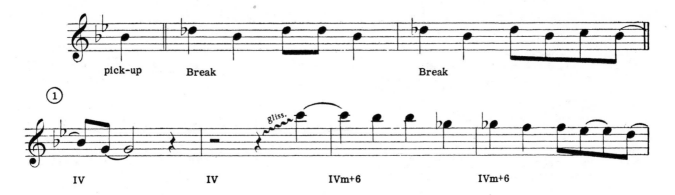

AFTER YOU'VE GONE—

VIx　　　　　　　　II　　　　　　　　IVm+6

I+6　　　　　　　　IIIx　　　　　　　　VI

#IVo　　　　　　　VI2　　　　　　VI2　　　V　　　　V

②

Break　　　　　Break　　　　　　Break　　　　Break
I+6　　　　　　　　　　　　　　　　　　　　　　　　　IV+6

IV+6　　　　　　　IVm+6　　　　　　IVm+6

I+6　　　　　　　　I+6　　　　　　　VIx　　　　　　VIx

IIx　　　　　　　　IIx　　　　　　　　V

V　　　　Break　　　　　　　　　Break
　　　　　I+6

Break　　　　　　　Break　　　　　IV+6　IV+6　　　　　IVm+6

IVm+6   I+6   I+6   VIx

VIx   II   VIx   II

IVm+6   I+6   IIIx

VI   #IVo   VI2   VI2

V   V   I+6   II   III #IVo

IVm+6   IVm+6   IIx V_3^4

Break   Break   Break

ritard.
Break   ♭VIx

V   ♭IIx   Ix   Ix

SWEET SUE — JUST YOU   TEDDY WILSON

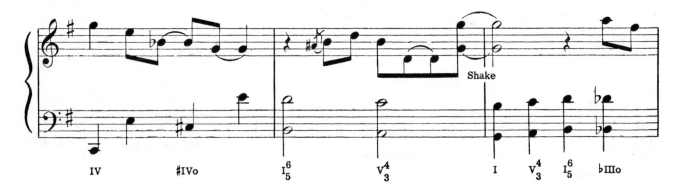

IV   III   ♭IIIo   V$^4_3$ I   ♭VIo   Ix$^4_3$ IV   ♯IVo

I$^4_3$ V$^4_3$ I   I$^4_3$ I$^6_5$

VIIx$^6_5$ ♭VIIx$^6_5$

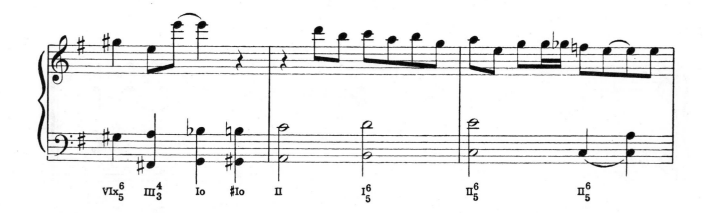

VIx$^6_5$ III$^4_3$ Io ♯Io   II   I$^6_5$ II$^6_5$ II$^6_5$

IVm   II∅   III   II∅$^6_5$ II∅

V$^4_3$ #Io   V$^4_3$ ♭IIIo   V$^4_3$ #Io   V$^4_3$ ♭IIIo

V$^4_3$ V   I   ♭VIo   Ix$^4_3$ IV   #IVo

Shake

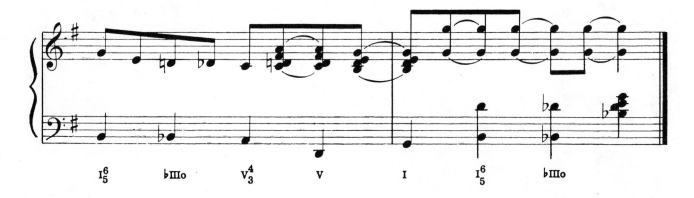

I$^6_5$ ♭IIIo   V$^4_3$ V   I   I$^6_5$ ♭IIIo

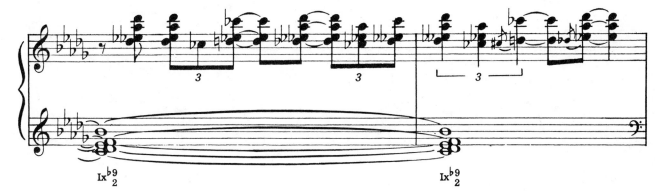

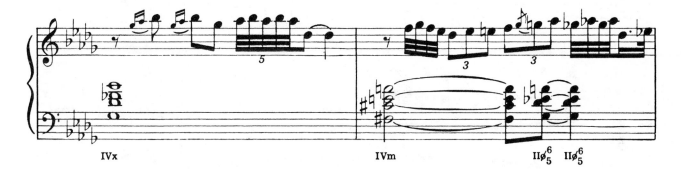

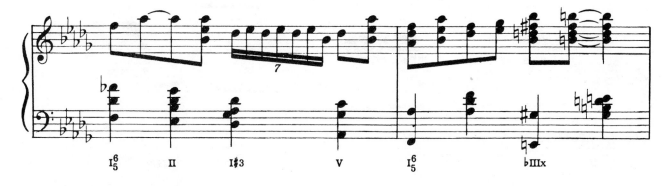

II — V — #Io II — IIIx IV — #IVo VI2 — IIx V V

I — Ix2 — IVx — ♭VIIx — I⁶₅ — IIx V — I

Ix♭⁹₂ — I — Ix♭⁹₂ Ix♭⁹₂ — Ix♭⁹₂ VIIx VIIx⁹₂

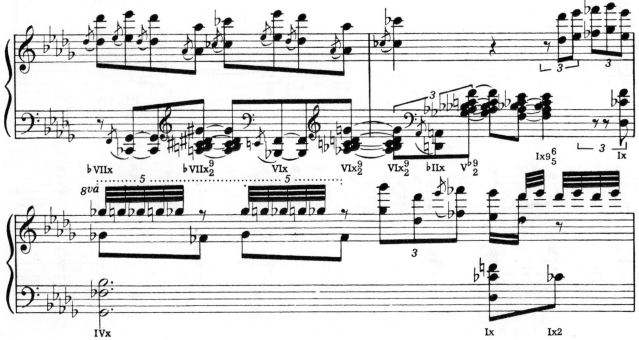

♭VIIx — ♭VIIx⁹₂ — VIx — VIx⁹₂ VIx⁹₂ ♭IIx V♭⁹₂ — Ix9⁶₅ Ix

IVx — Ix Ix2

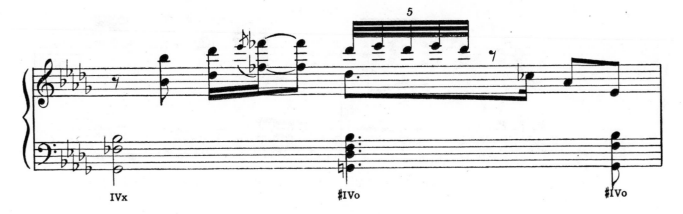

IVx   #IVo   #IVo

VI2   VI2   VI2

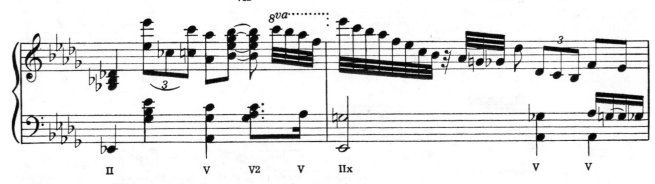

VI2   III   bIII

II   V   V2   V   IIx   V   V

I   IV   IV   III   bIII   II   V   V2

I II$^4_3$ VIIx I #I I II #IIo I$^6_5$ Im$^4_3$ VI∅$^4_3$ II∅ I

VII IIIx#5 VI ♭VIo VI2 VI ♭VIo VI2 ♭V∅ II$^6_5$ II2

VII IIIx VI ♭VI Vm ♭V ♭V♭5 IVx♭5 IVx♭5 Vm Ix IVo

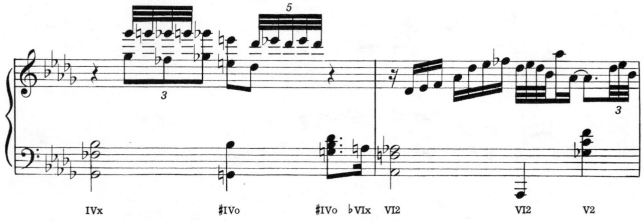

IVx #IVo #IVo ♭VIx VI2 VI2 V2

I^6_5 bIIIo

II bIIo

II V

I Ix IVx bVo bVo

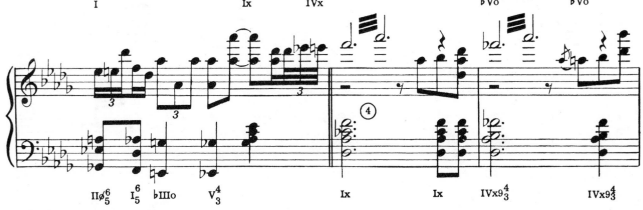

$II\emptyset^6_5$ I^6_5 bIIIo V^4_3 Ix Ix $IVx9^4_3$ $IVx9^4_3$

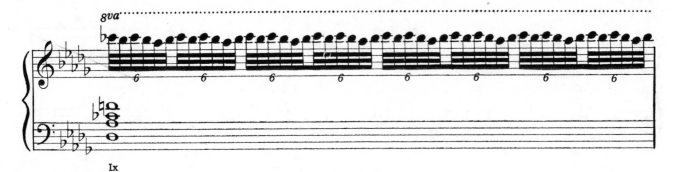

Ix

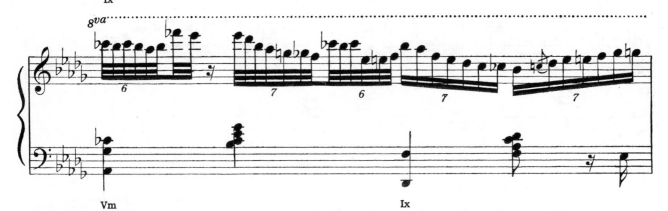

Vm   Ix

Im   IVx $IVx9_3^4$

IVx_3^4 IVx   IVm+6

I_5^6 I_3^4 I   I

I^6_5 VI2 #I   I   #I   #IV   V

V V$^4_3$ V   V   VI   VIx#5   IIx   V#3   Vb9   I   I

Coda

Ix^{b9}_2 Ix^{b9}_2 I Ix^{b9}_2 Ix^{b9}_2 I Ix^{b9}_2

Ix^{b9}_2 bIIx   Vb9   bVIx V I   Ix

IVx   bIIIM   II   bIIxb5   Ixb5   Ixb5

89

SOFT WINDS   BENNY GOODMAN

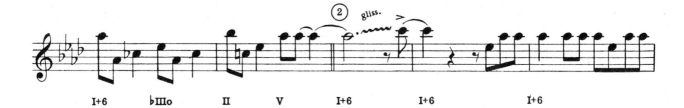

CRAZY RHYTHM

COLEMAN HAWKINS AND BENNY CARTER

Carter

II   V   I+6   I+6   I+6

I+6   V   V   I+6   VI

II   V   I+6   I+6   I+6   I+6

gliss.

V   V   I+6   I+6

Ix   Ix   IV   IV

IVm+6   ♭VIIx   III   VIx   II   V

I+6   VI   IIx   IIx   V

Carter

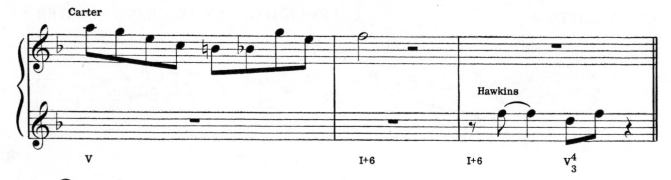

V   I+6   I+6 V^4_3

① **Hawkins**

I+6   I+6   I+6   I+6

V   V   I+6   VI   II   V   I+6

I+6   I+6   I+6   V

V   I+6   I+6   Ix

Ix   IV   IV   IVm+6

♭VIIx   III   VIx   II   V   I+6

VI   IIx   IIx   V   V

② Hawkins

I+6   I+6   I+6   I+6

I+6   I+6   V   V

I+6   VI   II   V   I+6   I+6

I+6   I+6   V   V

I+6   I+6   Ix   Ix

IV   IV   IVm+6   ♭VIIx

III   VIx   II   V   I+6   VI

IIx   IIx   II

Ensemble

V   I+6   V   I+6

PART 4
Early Progressive

JUST YOU, JUST ME   LESTER YOUNG

JUST YOU, JUST ME — Lyric by Raymond Klages — Music by Jesse Greer

V   3   Ix   IV+6   #IVo

VI2   V   I+6   V   I+6 $III\emptyset^4_3$

VIx   II   V   Ix

IV+6   #IVo   VI2   V   I+6

Ix   Ix   IV+6

bVIIx   I+6   VI

IIx   V   I+6 $III\emptyset^4_3$

VIx   II   V

Ix   IV+6   #IVo   VI2   V   I+6

I CAN'T GET STARTED

DIZZY GILLESPIE

(C)   II⌀   V♭5   I+6

(C)   I   (D) II   V   II   V

(D)   I   I

(C)   II   V♭5   II   V♭5

(C)   I   VIx♭9   II   V♭9   I   VI

(C)   II   V   IIIx   ♭IIIx

(C)   IIx   ♭IIx   I   VI   II   V♭5

CODA

(C)   III⌀   VIx♭5   II⌀

(C)   V♭5   V♭5   retard   ♭IIM   I

LADY BIRD (HALF NELSON)

(C)   I   I

(C)   IVm   ♭VIIx   I

(C)   I   VIIm   IIIx   (A♭) II   V

(A♭)   I   I

(C)   VI   IIx   II

(C)   V♭5   III   ♭IIIx

LADY BIRD (HALF NELSON) —
    Used by permission of Savoy Music Company, Newark, New Jersey.

(C)   ♭VIM   V♭5   I   I

(C)   IVm   ♭VIIx

(C)   I   I

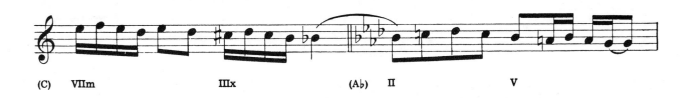

(C)   VIIm   IIIx   (A♭)   II   V

(A♭)   I   I   (C)   VI

(C)   IIx   II   V

(C)   I   ♭IIIx$^4_3$ ♭VIM   V   I

NICE WORK IF YOU CAN GET IT

BUD POWELL

VI   IIx   V   V

IIIx   VIx   IIx   V   I+6   VI

IIx   #IIo   III   VIx   II   V

III   VIx   II   V   I+6

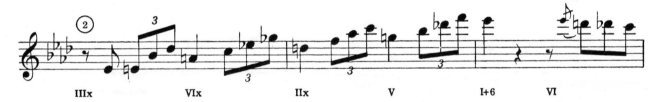

IIIx   VIx   IIx   V   I+6   VI

IIx   bIIo   III   VI   II   V

II   V   I+6   IIIx   VIx

IIx   V   I   VI   IIx   #IIo

III VIx II V̇   II   V

I+6 ♭VIIx VI   Im IVx

VI   IIx   Vm   IIIø

VI IIx   V   V

IIIx   VIx   IIx   V

I+6   VI   IIx   #IIo

III   VIx   II   V

III VIx   II   V   I+6

CHEROKEE (KO KO)

CHARLIE PARKER

(Bb) I+6   I+6   Vm

(Bb) Ix   IV   IV   IVm

(Bb) bVIIx   I   VI

(Bb) IIx   IIx   II

(Bb) bIIo   II   bIIx

(Bb) I+6   VI   II   V   Vm

(B♭)   IV   IV   IVm

(B♭)   ♭VIIx   I   VI

(B♭)   IIx   IIx   II

(B♭)   ♭IIx   I+6   I+6

(B)   II   ♭IIx   I   I

(A)   II   ♭IIx   I   I

(G)   II   ♭IIx   I   I

(B♭)   Vm   Ix   IV

(B♭)   IV   IVm   ♭VIIx

(B♭)   I   VI   IIx

(B♭)   IIx   II   VIx

(B♭)   II   V   I

(B♭)   I   Vm   Ix

(B♭)   IV   IV   IVm

(Bb)   bIIIx   I   VI

(Bb)   IIx   IIx   II   bIIx

(Bb)   I+6   I+6   (B)   II

(B)   bIIx   I   I

(A)   II   bIIx   I   I

(G)   II   II   V

(G)   I   I   (Bb) VI

(B♭) IIx   II   ♭IIx

(B♭) I   I

(B♭) Vm   Ix   IV

(B♭) IV   IVm   ♭VIIx

(B♭) I   VI   IIx

(B♭) IIx   II   ♭IIx

(B♭) I+6   I+6   I+6

JUST FRIENDS

CHARLIE PARKER

V   ♭V   IV   3

IV   3   ♭VIIx

♭VIIx   I   I   3

♭III   3   ♭VIx

II   3   3   V

IIIx   3   3   VI   3

IIx   3   II   ♭IIx   3   3   3

I   3   I

PART 5
Late Progressive

LOVER MAN

LEE KONITZ

(G)   ♭VIx   V   I

(A)   II##7   II#7

(A)   II   3   V   6

(A)   I   I   (G) II##7   II#7

(G)   II   V   I   3

(G)   VII   IIIx

(G)   VI   IIx

(G)   VI   IIx

(G)   II   V

(G)   II   V   Ix   Ix

(G)   IVx

(G)   ♭VIx   V   I

Release - last 16

(A)   II   II   V

(A)   I   I

113

(G)   II   V   II   V

(G)   I   VIIm   IIIx

(G)   VI   IIx   VI   IIx

(G)   II   II   V

(G)   Ix   IVx

(G)   ♭VIx   V   II

(G)   ♭IIx   Im^{+}6

ALL THE THINGS YOU ARE

CHET BAKER

ALL THE THINGS YOU ARE —

WRAP YOUR TROUBLES IN DREAMS

STAN GETZ

2nd Chorus

bV∅   VIIx   IIIx   VIx   IIx   V

I   I   I

V#5   I+6   IIIx   VI

IIx   IIx   II   V#3

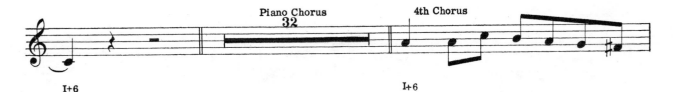

Piano Chorus
32
4th Chorus

I+6   I+6

V#5   I   IIIx   VI

IIx   IIx   II   V#3

I   I   V#5

I   IIIx   VI   IIx

IIx   II   V#5   I

♭V∅   VIIx   III∅   VIx

IIx   V   I   ♭V∅   VIIx

IIIx   VIx   IIx   V   I   V#5

I   V#5   I   IIIx

VI   IIx   IIx

II   V#5   I

118

I DON'T STAND A GHOST OF A CHANCE WITH YOU

CLIFFORD BROWN

Pick-up
V♭5   I

V♭5

Ix♭9   3   3   IVm   ♭VIIx

III   ♭IIIo   II   V♭9   IVo

III   VIx

II   IIø   V♭9

I   V♭5

I DON'T STAND A GHOST OF A CHANCE WITH YOU — Copyright 1932 by American
    Academy of Music, Inc.
    Used by permission.

Ixb9   IVm   bVIIx

III   bIIIo   II   V#3
                                                            9

I   I   #Io

II

V#5

I

I   bVø

VIIx

III   3   VIx

II   V♭5

I

V♭5

Ix

IVm   ♭VIIx

III   ♭IIIo   II   ♭IIx

I   V♭5   V♭5

OPUS DE FUNK   HORACE SILVER

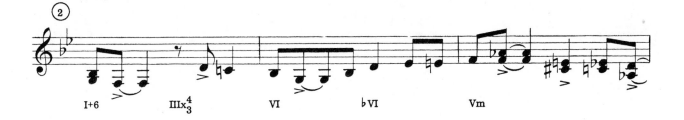

II · · · · V · · · · I+6 · · · · VI · · · · II · · · · V

I+6 · · · · VI · · · · Vm · · · · Ix · · · · IVx

#IVo · · · · VI2 · · · · IV · · · · III · · · · ♭III

II · · · · V · · · · VI2

VI2 · · · · I+6 · · · · #Io · · · · II · · · · #IIo

III · · · · ♭VI · · · · Vm · · · · Ix · · · · IVx

#IVo · · · · VI2 · · · · IV · · · · III · · · · ♭III

II · · · · II · · · · V · · · · I+6 · · · · VI · · · · II · · V

I+6   VI   II   V   I+6   Vm   Ix

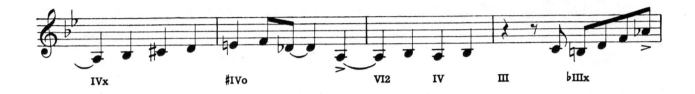

IVx   #IVo   VI2   IV   III   ♭IIIx

II   V   I+6   VI

II   V   I+6   IVx   I+6   ♭VI

Vm   Ix   IVx   #IVo

VI2   IV   III   ♭III   II

V   I+6   VI   II   V

I+6   VI   II   V   I+6   ♭VI

Vm   Ix   IVx   #IVo

VI2   IV   III   ♭III   II

V   I+6   VI   II   V

I+6   VI   II   V   I   ♭VI

Vm   Ix   IVx   #IVo

VI2   IV   III   ♭III   II

V   I+6   VI   II   ♭IIx   Ixb9

127

VI2   IV   III   bIIIx   II Ix_5^6 IV

#IVo   VI2   VI2   VI2

IV   #IVo   IVm   III

VIx   II VI_3^4 IVx #IVo VI2   V

I+6   I+6   Ix#11   Ix#11

Ix#11   b5

128

I'VE GOT THE WORLD ON A STRING

OSCAR PETERSON

INTRO
♭VIIx   VIx   ♭VIIx   VIx

II   IIø⁶₅

III   ♭III

II   ♭VIx   V

I+6   ♭VIIx   VIx   II   V

I   IVx   III   ♭III   II   V

II   V   ♭VIIx   VIx   ♭VIx

♭VIx   V   I+6   VIx

II   V   I   IVx

III   ♭III   II   V

II   V   I+6

I+6   VIIm

IIIx   VIx

VIx   IIx

IIx   II

II   V   I+6   VIx

II   V   I   IVx

III   ♭III   II

II   V   I+6   Break

Break   1+6   ♭VIIx   VIx

II   V   I   IVx

III VIx II II

II V IIIx VIx

IIx V I+6 VIx

II V I+6 IVx

III ♭III II V

II V

I+6 IVx I+6

VIIm · · · · · · · · IIIx

VIx · · · · · · · · VIx

IIx · · · · · · · · IIx

♭III · · · · · ♭VIx · · · · · II · · · · · V

I+6 · · · · · VIx · · · · · II · · · · · V

I+6 · · · · · IVx · · · · · III · · · · · ♭III

II · · · · · II · · · · · V · · · · · I+6 · · · · · VIx

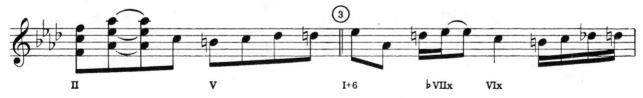

II · · · · · V · · · · · I+6 · · · · · ♭VIIx · · · VIx

133

II   V   I+6   IVx

III   ♭IIIo   II

II   V   IIIx   VIx

♭III   II   V   I+6   VIx

II   V   I+6   IVx

III   ♭III   II

II   V   I+6   IVx

I+6   IIIx   IIIx

VIx   VIx

IIx   IIx

V   3   3   V

I+6   VIx   II   V

I+6   IVx   III   bIII

II   II   V

I+6   VIx   IIx   V

⑤

Pick-up   I+6   VIx   II   V

I+6   IVx   III   ♭III

II   II   V

IIIx   VIx   IIx   V

      #Io   #IIo
I+6   VIx   II   V   I+6   IVx

III   ♭III   II   V

II   V   I+6

I+6   IIIx

IIIx   VIx

VIx   IIx

IIx   6   6

V

V   V   I+6   VIx

II   V   I+6   IVx

III   bIII   II   V

II   V   I+6   bVIIo   VI$^{4}_{3}$ V$^{4}_{3}$

137